I Sit Listening to the Wind

Reviews of *I SIT LISTENING TO THE WIND*

An invitation to the magic inner circle . . .

"Written with sound Jungian psychology and gentle intuitiveness, yet stirred by assertiveness, Duerk invites us into that magic inner circle of the Feminine Mystique, urging us to use the Masculine energy productively and wisely. Highly recommended."—*Spiritual Studies Center Booknews*

An encouragement to be inwardly reflective . . .

"A nourishing, tenderly understanding, helpful book about the Masculine within women that encourages readers to be inwardly attentive and reflective."—Jean Shinoda Bolen, M.D., Author of *Goddesses in Everywoman* and *Crossing to Avalon*

Harmony to live by . . .

"In contrast to feminists who talk about rights to fight for, Judith Duerk talks about harmony to live by. *I Sit Listening to the Wind* speaks of a different way for the next generation, the daughters of the women who give voice to their experiences in Judith's book."—Edith Wallace, M.D., Ph.D., Jungian Analyst; Author of *A Queen's Quest: Pilgrimage for Individuation*

Gently powerful and healing . . .

"Again, Judith Duerk shows us that there is a path of our own that we can follow to find a way of encountering the Masculine side of ourselves. The intimacy of the imagery and the feminine quality of her presentation makes her writing unique . . . gently powerful . . . healing."—Kay Bradway, Ph.D., Founding Member of the C.G. Jung Institute of San Francisco; Author of *Villa of Mysteries* and Co-author of *Sandplay: Silent Workshop of the Psyche*

A book you'll read again and again . . .

"Written in [a] meditative mixture of prose, poetry, and reflective questions . . . this is a quiet, passionate book you'll be reading again and again."—*Chinaberry Catalog*

Auditory training for the soul . . .

"*I Sit Listening to the Wind* attunes a third ear to hear faint musings of awareness, screeches of outrage, tears of loss, and gleanings of wisdom. Duerk coaxes them into consciousness with respect for the Feminine experience. Auditory training for the soul."—Christella Carbaugh, SLW, Coordinator of Spiritual Life, Sisters of the Living Work

An essential book for women . . .

"Judith models the best of Feminine Persuasion, a meditative invitation for the reader to attune to the Deepest Authority: HerSelf."—Christina Baldwin, Author of *Calling the Circle: The First and Future Culture* and Co-founder of Peer Spirit Circling

A primer for becoming fully yourself . . .

"A valuable primer for a woman seeking to become fully herself. Step by step Judith Duerk leads us through the struggle to realize a balanced life, as we vie with those two great forces, the Feminine and the Masculine. Using the voices of many women, she draws us into real life experience. In the company of these women, we find a mirror for the passage we call our own."—Betty De Shong Meador, Ph.D., Jungian Analyst; Author of *Uncursing the Dark*

A call to take time to listen . . .

"How many times in the busyness of our lives do we take time to listen to the wind? This book is the reflection of one woman who took time to be with herself and discovered a new source of time—Kairos . . . sacred time."—*Crone Chronicles*

CIRCLE OF STONE SERIES

BY JUDITH DUERK

CIRCLE OF STONES
Woman's Journey To Herself

I SIT LISTENING TO THE WIND
Woman's Encounter Within Herself

THE CIRCLE CONTINUES
Women Respond to Circle of Stones

I sit listening to the wind

woman's encounter within herself

JUDITH DUERK

to the wind

INNER OCEAN PUBLISHING, INC.

Inner Ocean Publishing, Inc.
P.O. Box 1239
Makawao, Maui, HI 96768-1239
www.innerocean.com

Originally published by Innisfree Press, Inc.

Publisher Cataloging-in-Publication Data
Duerk, Judith.
I sit listening to the wind : woman's encounter within herself / by
Judith Duerk. — Makawao, HI : Inner Ocean, 2005, c1999.
p. ; cm.
(Circle of stones series ; v. 2)
Previously published: Philadelphia : Innisfree Press, 1999.
ISBN: 1-880913-65-8
1. Women—Psychology. 2. Women—Identity. 3. Femininity.
4. Identity (Psychology) 5. Sex role. I. Title.
HQ1206 .D84 2005
155.3/33—dc22 0502

DISTRIBUTED BY PUBLISHER'S GROUP WEST

For information on promotions, bulk purchases, premiums, or educa-
tional use, please contact: 866.731.2216 or sales@innerocean.com.

Acknowledgments

My acknowledgment to LuraMedia, who originally published this material, and to Marcia Broucek of Innisfree Press for her perseverance and dedication. Most recently, my hearty appreciation to Karen Bouris and Alma Bune of Inner Ocean Publishing for their help with this present volume.

My thanks to the women who have granted the use of their dreams and writings and to the circles of women everywhere who have given encouragement as this book has progressed.

to

the memory

of a woman

who struggled

to

bring forth

herself

Contents

How might your life have been different if, once, as a young girl, you had wandered alone in the woodlands not far from your mother's home . . . and you had come upon a small glade you had never seen before?

If you had listened to the wind blow mysteriously . . . had seen, there in the shadows, a group of rough-hewn stones, gathered in a circle . . . and, somehow, you knew that this was a place where women gathered throughout the ages to reflect upon their lives?

And, if, as you sat down on one of the stones, you could feel the presence of those women reaching out to welcome you . . .

How might your life be different?

Preface

I sit listening, the wind blows. An image comes to me of a woman in a moment of reflection, sitting quietly to listen within. She listens to her own Feminine feelings and perceptions, but also to her inner Masculine side, in wonder at its energy and what it stirs within her. She senses with an ancient sense the work that is hers to do to develop herself and her gifts, seeking to hold her ground and not be blown away.

Then, in her individual way, she enters a life-long encounter as she engages with this Masculine energy, which spiritual traditions throughout the ages have characterized as "The Wind." It is the Masculine/Yang energy within a woman's Feminine/Yin psyche. It brings her focus and energy to grow into her wholeness as a woman.

Jung called this Masculine energy within a woman's psyche the "animus."

I think of the cycles of a woman's life, of early bonding with the mother, then ideally, through that bond, her grounding in the Archetypal Feminine, and underneath that, roots in the deeper Self. Then the awakening of her Masculine energy as she fulfills her achievement side, schooling, and professional life, perhaps marriage and children.

These are years of great possibility for a woman, of consciously seeking the help of her animus to focus on Feminine values and bring them to expression in her life. In a complete absence of animus energy, there is no life, the air is dead. The woman is unable to focus and develop, her gifts lie dormant within.

But for many modern women, that Masculine is ever there, ever blowing, filling any space left empty when she fails to know her individual feelings or define her values, filling it with judgments and criticisms from society around her. If she does not know what she personally stands for, the animus will operate autonomously, preaching his collective standards instead of helping the woman focus on her subjective truth. And her Feminine values will remain unspoken!

Even as I write these words, I am aware of a voice. "This book is neither definitive nor authoritative. It is too subjective to be of any consequence. Mostly," says the voice, "everyone knows all of this already."

"And besides, it's a trifle boring!"

I smile. How like the animus within a woman to end with a little swipe, "And haven't you put on a bit of weight?"

The animus does not want to be revealed as he really is, but capers around the room distracting me in a dozen directions. He creeps in, wordy and pompous, then strident and obnoxious, with grandiose proclamations. These paragraphs were begun to explore the dismissing voices of a woman's animus as she struggles to listen within and to bring forth her own perceptions. *And, even as I write of the dismissing voices, a voice dismisses me!*

❖ ❖ ❖

There is a deep pathos in women today with our highly developed animus. The nature of the Yin/Feminine is to yield, the nature of the Yang/Masculine to dominate. The two are forever equal and necessary to complete the wholeness of the cosmos. We modern women with our powerful inner Yang side are faced with an enormous task: to ground ourselves so thoroughly in the vibrant receptivity of the Yin, that we do not succumb to the compelling insistence of the Yang within us.

For if we lack the steadiness to remain rooted in the Feminine, we lose our connection through it to the Self within. We abdicate completely to an animus mode and accommodate to the standards of the collective. When women are taken over by their inner Yang side, or men by their inner Yin, they go to extreme measures to conform to "the group," leaving behind their individual relationship with the deeper Self.

Surely this pattern needs to be broken, particularly in these critical times when the deepest possible wisdom is needed!

The world is crying out for a developed Feminine voice. A voice that can mediate, once again, the ancient values of the Feminine: values of interiority, of the sacredness of nature and matter, values that honour the privacy of individual process . . . the values of the deeper Self held within us all.

In our efforts to effect change in our society, women to-day may not realize that we leave unexplored the Feminine modes that might accomplish the same ends if we could redis-cover them: modes of holding within ourselves our vision of what could be, gestating it with a spiritual energy that is uniquely Feminine, and finally bringing forth that vision in a circumspect womanly voice.

There is a story of canaries, valued for their sensitivities, taken below the surface in old mines to test for poison gas. We women are sometimes accused of being over-sensitive. Yet, the entire world today is in desperate need of women of sensitivity and clarity who can point out what is poisonous just below the surface. Women who have grounded themselves, developed their vision and voice, and can identify what is twisted in society today . . . women with the courage to speak out for their subjective values, who will take a stand for individual truth.

In my writing, I speak often of daughters, but I do not mean biological daughters. I am fiercely proud of my sons and of their Masculine energy. Yet, there is a distinctly Feminine spiritual energy, an energy that flows from the Archetypal Great Mother herself.

How can we women of today open ourselves to this ancient flow . . . let it flow through us to our daughters,

to the women of the future . . .

to the daughters of all of us?

Her Grounding
IN THE FEMININE

A *sense of time*

I sit listening to the wind . . .
. . . the woods are cool and quiet.

The wind blows . . . brings a memory from many years ago:

The storms of early autumn had felled large trees and branches in the woods nearby. For several days the men had worked to clear away the timber. The firewood had been cut in lengths and neatly stacked to dry. What was left was in a heap of tangled brush and twigs. It was an eyesore, in the way, and in the very place I had wanted to write for the next few days.

There was no one else to clean it up, so I started with a vengeance, intending to make short shrift of it and get on with my real work. For a few hours I laboured furiously, pulling at the pile, grabbing at the ends of the largest branches, trying to disentangle the heap by sheer brute force and my accumulated animosity. I learned later that a young woodsman had returned, willing to work, but had fled in fright before the ferocity of my face and efforts.

By late morning, it was clear that nothing effective was happening. My petulant tearings and rippings at the pile finally began to slow down. Much of my irritation had worn itself off . . . the woods had worked its way.

I stopped to sit on a nearby rock and knew that I must eat.

When I went back to work, it was with a different energy . . . no longer impatiently pulling at the protruding limbs or trying to overturn the heap. With clippers, I began to trim whatever offered itself from the stack. In my agitation of the morning, I had not seen that it could be approached in this way.

By late afternoon, I knew there was no way that the task would be finished that day. I began to work more slowly to sink into my experience with the brush. To the right went branches, neatly stacked, ready for drying or burning. To the left, I placed little bundles of twigs to be used later as kindling.

As the shadows lengthened, a quieter rhythm emerged. The task seemed more worthy of itself . . . my real work, less pressing. I stopped before I grew too tired and, much to my surprise, began to write, as I had first intended, right there beside the brush.

On the morning of the second day, I awakened early with a sense of eagerness, not to finish the job of clearing, but to see what the day might bring if I offered myself to the task. At intervals I rested, with no clear plan for what must be completed that day. It was almost no surprise to find myself writing in the woods as I rested.

The day passed.

Near the middle of the third day, I became aware of something wondrous happening. My whole experience was shifting . . . the molecules of time, itself, opened up before me, spreading themselves apart so that there was space and breadth amongst them . . . breath to breathe within each moment.

I laid down the clippers and sat on the rock to sense the moment more fully, as I had not allowed myself to do the day before.

I saw the wind in the tallest trees slowly stir the leaves. The colours shifted from darkest greens to black . . . to nearly yellow. A hush was in the woods around, as well as deep within, me. I watched there, while the sun set, then walked silently to the house.

I washed my hair and did the few things necessary to prepare for the coming week.

The next morning, as the fourth day dawned, the whole house lay in quietness. The preparations of the evening before, undertaken out of the silence, had emerged from a sense of ordering far deeper than conscious planning. What had not been done never would be missed.

When I returned to the woods to work, I carried a broom with the clippers. By noontime, all of the remaining twigs had been put into the little bundles and tied with yarn from the house, for there was no twine. I swept the ground where the brush had been, smoothing out the last bits of bark. The earth lay flat and clean again . . . the grass, a pale yellow.

The wind blows . . . I sit listening against a tree.

Many times, through the years, I have remembered that day. There was a sense of being deep within the doing. Rather than a driven way of pressing to complete the task, knowing every second what the next ten thousand would hold, it was as if I had slipped through a scrim into a timeless, mysterious realm . . . silent . . . shimmering with life.

One whole day of being, not in ordinary Chronos time, but in the sacred Kairos time of the Feminine realm. I had glimpsed a way of being in which time, itself, was sentient, quivering with its own awareness of what each moment could hold.

One moment, I had been trapped by time, cut off from myself. In the next moment, time itself was alive, connecting me to my feelings, to all things in the circle of life . . . to a way of being, from long ago when the earth was still held sacred. When a woman knew that her task was necessary to the cycles of nature. Knew that her devotion within, as she fulfilled the task, reconsecrated the earth and echoed throughout the cosmos.

I lean against the tree, thinking of our needs as women. Our ordinary lives are no longer lived in nature. It is difficult, in daily life, to find the Feminine realm. The drawing of the water, the gathering of the grains no longer are performed under an open sky. Even the machines that assist a woman prevent her from holding the elemental in her hands. The sense of her task as consecrated and necessary to the cosmos is gone.

And I fear for women yet to come. For under the pressures of modern life, time has become compressed. The Feminine sense of time has all but disappeared. Yet woman cannot exist with only a linear awareness of time, for her sense of sacred Kairos time is the precious essence of life. There must be time enough for her to experience the sacredness within each moment and within herself.

How can woman redeem what was lost so long ago? For millennia, as she was defined by man, woman developed herself in the prevailing Masculine image. But the heroic journey of the Masculine, so long clearly delineated, could not provide what was needed to complete the journey of the conscious and developed Feminine. It could not help woman return to her Archetypal roots or to the sacredness of her sense of Kairos time.

The locust tree at my back sways. I sit, trying to understand the shift in my experiencing of time. What had made time so alive? Yet, even as I try so purposefully to comprehend the shift, wondering, perhaps, if I might make it happen, the precious aliveness dies. It cannot be made to happen!

Finally I sit empty, waiting.

❖ ❖ ❖

A single shaft of blinding sunlight pierces through the leaves . . . onto the bundles of twigs lying at my feet . . . touches the pages of my writing. I hold my breath as a thousand tiny sprinkles of light fill the air above. It could not be made to happen. Yet it is happening once more!

Time is alive again!

I sit listening to the wind . . . and I wonder how to be willing to offer myself into each moment . . . into *this* moment, now. How to give over, humbly, to the sovereignty, to the utter autonomy this moment seems to ask. How to let myself and the moment slip through the mysterious scrim
       . . . from the purposeful and known
        . . . to the timeless.

The leaves fall
       . . . Time drifts by.

How might your life have been different if, when you felt time pressing in on you, there were a place to go where you were allowed to simply be? If, as you sat down silently, there were a sense of the presence of other women breathing in the stillness . . . waiting quietly with you?

And if you watched the dappled shadows on the ground around you as the wind suddenly stilled . . . and you entered a new sense of time, of time stretching out before you?

And you knew that there would finally be time enough for you . . .

How might your life be different?

A sense of identity

> *I sit listening . . .*
> *. . . the wind blows.*

An old woman sits with me . . . watches as the aspen leaves flutter to the ground . . . speaks of a past struggle:

"We entered, all alone, into the unknown . . . with little to support or sustain us from a familiar realm. There was no way a woman could succeed but to give up parts of herself!

"I was one of the few women at the conservatory when it was announced that a master class would be given by a woman of great renown. There were stories of superb artistry, as well as imprisonment and narrow escape in the war. Her concert the evening before the class brought tumultuous applause.

"I wondered at her appearance the next morning, as she walked across the stage: she carried a brown leather satchel, worn-looking, with a frayed handle . . . settled her materials on a small table, rather than on the podium standing imposingly alongside. One could see her frailness. Yet her presence filled the concert hall in a way I had not seen before.

"She requested a glass of water and asked to be certain that those in the audience, waiting with impatience, were comfortable. The last thing she did, before she began to teach, was to cross over to where her brown satchel sat on the floor. She took out a faded, rose-coloured sweater, which she put on over her elegant gown. There was a small hole at the left elbow.

"She said the hall felt a little drafty.

"The audience, candidates for graduate degrees, had arrived well before she came. There were professors and dignitaries from hundreds of miles around. The woman was to teach a handful of student performers chosen by the faculty. The class began quietly. The woman artist tried to put the young musicians at ease. She spoke of willingly submitting one's skill and mastery to bringing forth the pathos and meaning from the heart of the music itself."

The old woman sighs, then continues:

"It was what happened at the close of the day that has lingered with me for so long. In the customary question period, the students and scholars became caught up in outdoing one another. Several extremely technical questions were briefly but thoroughly answered. Then, as sometimes happens on these occasions, a fever fell over the auditorium. The questions became abstract and belaboured.

"In her steady way, the woman artist began to turn away the questions. 'No,' she said to this one, 'that denies the spirit of the day.' 'No,' to another, 'I am not an expert in that area, but perhaps,' she wondered, 'might there be someone in the audience who is?' After several more questions had been turned away, the woman expressed concern that the soul of the music was being lost.

"There was a rustle of unrest. The questions abruptly ceased. The dean of the conservatory thanked the woman artist and brought the master class to a close. As the audience emptied down the aisle and out the rear door, the woman crossed over again to where the worn, brown satchel sat on the floor. She folded her sweater into it.

A sense of identity

"Several of the young women performers lingered on the stage . . . tried to engage the woman again in questions. She answered only one, with the simplest and briefest of answers . . . then started to say that she was tired. But the questioners had already left, in haste and disappointment.

"I saw there were two more young women still waiting in the shadows. One asked if she might help the woman artist with the satchel. She looked very surprised . . . hesitated for a moment. Then she quietly asked if they would like to join her for a cup of tea while she waited for her train."

The wind blows . . . leaves fall more quickly around us as the old woman speaks:

"I have wondered, all these years, at the presence that woman had, there at the close of the day. She knew so truly who she was and the value of what she gave. She did not make herself give more. I am afraid my own tendency would have been so different, young, then, as I was, and eager for success!

"All day, before an erudite audience, she had reached out with her warm generativity to inspire the younger musicians, offered her consummate artistry. Then, as the late afternoon faded into evening, she entered another realm.

"That one moment has influenced profoundly my whole life as a woman. It was as if I felt the very ground underneath me shift. I glimpsed for the very first time that other realm a woman might choose in which to live her life . . . a different mode to bring meaning to her than goal-directed accomplishment."

The old woman reaches out her hand . . . catches a leaf as it falls:

"All these years, I have wondered, what became of those young women . . . the first two, so disappointed that the woman artist refused to be other than she was. And the courage of those last two who remained . . . while all the others left!

"I have wondered if they could see, already at their age, the choices she had made: her brilliant development in the Yang realm yet her grounded return to the Yin? I hoped the intelligence and grace with which she fulfilled her task might help those young women strike their own roots in that Feminine ground."

I sit listening to the wind, in wonder at its power to freshen or devastate. In wonder, also, at the Masculine energy working in a woman that can enliven her development or completely dominate it . . . Can help her recognize her worth, or keep her from ever knowing who she truly is.

The wind blows
. . . blows.
Leaves fall.

How might your life have been different if, as a young woman, struggling to find out who you were, you had known of a special place that helped you ground yourself? If you had pulled your warmest sweater from the hook beside the door . . . and set off, all alone.

And, as you walked in the gathering dusk down the loneliest part of your path, you felt the chill of evening . . . and drew your sweater more closely around you . . . until, finally, as you drew nearer to that special place, you stopped and stood quietly breathing in the stillness.

And the silence and the darkness helped you be present to yourself.

How might your life be different?

A sense of sustenance

The wind blows . . .
. . . chill and wild.

I put a log on the fire, glad to be warm and safe, thankful for this time of quiet to reconnect with myself. I remember another winter evening, long ago, when I sat quietly by the fire. My sons were very young then and slept peacefully in the next room.

That evening, for the first time, I had read of an experiment that left a deep impression on me, of baby monkeys given a choice between a wire or soft mother. The wire figure had a mechanical apparatus that dispensed a feeding . . . the soft form only a cushioned lap and pillowed body to lean against. The babies who survived best were those who chose the "soft mother."

Sitting alone there, that night, I wondered if my sons would allow themselves to choose the soft mother in their lives. Had I given them enough nurture for them to know what truly would sustain them? Enough elemental holding and touching to know how to care for their lives? Now, many years later, I sit in the stillness again . . . and as I watch the fire, I think of our lives and of the lives of women today . . . of the myriad choices open to us.

The wind blows an icy blast . . .
. . . drives sleet against the window.

I shiver as I consider the changes in the last few generations. Our grandmothers did not have the opportunities open to women now. If a woman wanted or needed to hold a position outside the home, she had to present herself in a Masculine image. There was little conscious awareness of the Archetypal Feminine. Women undervalued themselves and the nurturing roles they filled. Only the wire mother was known.

The tea in the heavy brown cup warms my hands. As I sort through the complexity of the changes for women, I am grateful to be brought back to my body. It is so easy to be pulled into our heads, into worry and inner argument.

When that happens, we women are so vulnerable to the animus and to his constant judging. It always seems unfair to me that the more a woman has sought to develop her animus, the more it tends to dominate the choices she makes in life. It can make her work unrelentingly to fulfill its heady ambitions, rather than helping her make a life that belongs to her . . . always choosing the wire mother that cannot nourish her.

A young woman speaks: *"I am so confused as I try to sort things out. As long as I work extended hours and have no time to reflect or feel, I can endure my life. After all, I tell myself, I've more than fulfilled my mother's rules:*

Keep all your options open.
Make only goal-directed choices.

"But when I overhear other women talking about their lives, I feel scared and hollow. They seem to settle into their lives in a way I've never allowed myself as I struggle to keep all my options open.

"I feel a longing for a woman's life I have never known, that my mother never knew, either. In my very worst moments, I grasp frantically at all my citations and awards, trying to draw comfort from anything, from anywhere at all."

❖ ❖ ❖

The second woman to speak is a little older than the first: *"Everything in my childhood had been a reflection of things outside ourselves, the house, the neighborhood, even the friends. Everything was chosen for appearances. Nothing to nourish me.*

"A few months ago, a position of more power and prestige had been offered to me and I was afraid my husband thought I should accept it. An old voice inside me said it was imperative to move ahead and I wanted to be sure where that voice came from. Was it really my husband's?

"I wanted to sort things out and be listened to by women's ears, so I went to my mother and sister. But they wouldn't hear my pain. I can still hear my mother's strident voice, 'You have no right to hold your husband back!'

"Somehow I got home from the encounter, feeling like a terrible failure. I had just enough energy left to put on my faded blue robe. As I sat and closed my eyes, I realized how barren the lives of my mother and sister were. I felt a wave of sadness for us all. My mother, so unable to acknowledge my pain and my need for nurture, because her own had never been acknowledged. My sister and I, never helped to embrace ourselves or our ordinary lives.

"Oh, if only my husband knew how I questioned the whole idea of this more important job, of being away so much, abandoning the intimacy of the life I had finally found

   . . . how much our mornings meant to me
    . . . the special quality of quietness in the
     empty, dark kitchen
      . . . soft flutter of wings at the feeder
       . . . the rustle of pages in my journal.

Suddenly I knew how to say it so he would be able to hear me."

An older woman nods and speaks: *"For many years, I met with a small group of women. We all had demanding jobs, but we made time to gather every month. Often, as we met, the woman who led us asked us to stop our restless spiritual discussions with their lofty quotations and to just breathe and be with ourselves. Once, at the end of a day, she asked us movingly to simply be together as women and share with each other the experiences of our ordinary lives.*

"When we gathered the next month, two of the women had been ill. It was the time of the winter solstice . . . the darkest days of the year.

"As we entered the room the woman had prepared, we all seemed to walk more slowly. The light from the windows was almost gone. The room became silent. We sat for a long while in the soft light from the candles and the fire on the hearth. At last we found within ourselves a quieter, darker place we had not known was there.

"One woman after another, we shared our struggle against emptiness, our need to keep busy to avoid despair ... our longings for a way of life that could nurture and sustain us."

"As the grey light at the windows grew fainter,
the room became hushed and still . . .
the candles burned low,
one woman fell asleep
the wind hummed low in the chimney."

How might your life have been different if there had been a place for you to go when your life was difficult and you felt utterly alone . . . a place of safety and comfort?

If a woman whom you trusted had been there to receive you . . . had listened silently, as you spoke your discouragement? And then she had covered you warmly as you curled up for a rest.

And, if she had gone out and returned with an armload of wood . . . then quietly built up the fire and sat down nearby to tend it . . .

How might your life be different?

A sense of voice

Late winter . . .
. . . the wind blows.

An image from a woman's dream drifts through the cold to me:

> *"A woman stands alone . . . watches the snow drift down. She is holding an egg, the precious and vulnerable symbol of her subjective truth as a woman. From nowhere, a man appears and seizes the egg from her. Identifying it as a football, and as his, at that, he darts down the field with it, dashing it heedlessly against a goal post. The man scores his points, but annihilates the living content of the woman's egg."*

How quickly our truth as women can be torn away from us! We may be completely unaware of how competitively we wage a discussion, how heedlessly we score points to dominate conversation. And whenever a new understanding of life emerges within us, rather than our silently holding it and pondering it in our hearts, it is stolen and broadcast to those around us.

This is the way of the animus. For the animus has little respect for our womanly understanding of life, and no ability to express our subtlety. As we begin to speak of our experiences and views, the animus crowds in. He states our material in bold terms, not caring for the sensitivity of our own womanly feelings or the feelings of those around us.

A woman speaks earnestly of this:

"When I listened to the recording of the faculty meeting, I heard, as I spoke, all that I have rejected in outer authorities from my past: everything as a complete certainty rather than with the nuance and subtlety that I am capable of. It was not my Feminine ego leading the meeting at all, but my animus in a skirt.

"The faces around the table came back to me, both the men and the women put off by the masculinized caricature of myself. Feeling ashamed and guilty, I remembered how little voice I had in the past and forgave my strident mode. Perhaps it had seemed better than having no voice at all.

"I wanted a new voice of constancy and prevailing, the qualities I wished to affirm in the teachers under my direction. I wanted to speak firmly as a woman of strength with my ego grounded in the Feminine. Slowly I worked with my convictions, solidifying here, softening there.

"Gradually I was filled with the feelings I had pushed away, with how much I cared for the work and the children we teachers all loved. The morning of the next meeting, I laid the agenda aside and prayed I could speak from my heart."

A second woman speaks:

"Although I knew I had grown, I still did not reach the women I addressed. I could hear myself begin sentences from within, and then listen helplessly while my animus finished each sentence in a masculine mode. He spoke to the women so cleverly that only their Masculine side was engaged.

"I felt disappointed and uncertain. All the quiet reflectiveness and depth within me so uncommunicated! I had sounded like the grandmother we were all taught to imitate, still stylish and slender at *ninety, with a crisp and amusing style . . . and always certain she was right. I knew I needed a mentor to help me find a truer voice.*

"The woman was older than I and very different from our family women. She asked me to respect my uncertainty, to be patient with it, and not to impose anything more on myself from the outside: Maybe that crisp and clever style could express your grandmother's nature, but is not capable of expressing yours.

"I have begun to let my uncertainty speak. What is emerging is not swift and clever, but not as slow and ponderous as I feared. And women seem to hear and respond to what is real in what I say."

A third woman sits in reflection before she begins to speak:

"My own experience has been so different, perhaps because I am older. I had begun to write of our individuation process as women. Acquaintances asked how the work was progressing and asked if they might see it.

"After only a few pages were read, the protests quickly began: Very nice work, indeed, but it must be reframed. The line is too fine, too lunar. It must be bolder, more declarative. It needs a completely different voice!

"Footsteps retreated down the driveway . . . car doors slammed shut.

"That weekend I lay in bed with flu, feverish and lost. The outer situation mirrored the chaos within . . . a female cardinal flew against the window, hour after hour, with a dull thud.

"My heart hurt under my ribs, and if I had not known so well how my body has always expressed my emotional pain, I would have

feared that I was suffering a heart attack. With the fever, scenes of failure from my whole life passed before my eyes. 'Weighed in the balances and found wanting,' thundered my old inner judges . . . 'the wrong mode . . . the wrong way . . . wrong.' As wrong-headed as that lady cardinal hurtling herself against the window.

"As I neared the very bottom of the chaos, I heard only the last sentence from several days before: 'It needs a different voice . . . a completely different voice.'

"My heart grew quieter. With the grey dawn came a solitary whisper . . . 'But this is my voice!' I had laboured so long to develop its steadfast measure and balance, worked so diligently to quietly bring it forth. This was the only voice I had. There was no other.

"I slept.

"In the days that followed, I chastised myself many times. Why was I not more forthright, bolder, as the acquaintances asked? Why was I . . . only as I was? And then a memory came of a painful, patriarchal attitude: An attitude that invalidates a woman whenever she seeks to express her subtle awareness as woman . . . leaves her struggling to bring forth her subjective experience in a hull of objectivity, an empty shell of words.

" 'No wonder,' I thought, 'that a woman sometimes adopts a Masculine voice as she speaks. No wonder she loses touch with her most poignant feeling values. And, worst of all, no wonder that a woman so often speaks her truth in a voice that is not her own . . . leaves her deepest Feminine wisdom mute, unvoiced, unheard.'

"The flu lingered several days. At last I felt well enough to be back in the woods one afternoon towards dusk. The light was soft . . . the late-winder woods, subtle hues of browns and greys.

"I sat for a long time watching the branches silhouetted against the darkening sky. Slowly, a tired awareness emerged within me . . . that all I wanted to do in my lifetime was to try . . . try to speak my truth as woman . . . to say it in my own voice."

I sit listening to the wind.
. . . the wind listens back to me.

A sense of voice

How might your life have been different if, as a young woman struggling to find your voice . . . in despair that you might never be able to say what you knew inside . . . there had been a place for you to begin to speak as a woman?

If you had been received into a circle of women, and during the silence, the women had let you speak . . . had let you speak over and over, as your words slowly came together . . . if they had listened deeply and attentively to your emerging voice?

And, how might it have been different for you, if you had seen, that day, in the faces of the women sitting there in the circle . . . in the still older faces of the women standing slightly behind them in the shadows . . . the pride and respect they felt as they heard your young woman's voice?

How might your life be different?

A sense of sacredness

The wind softens . . .
. . . winter thaws.

In earliest springtime of each year, a group of women gathered in a small mountain town where there was a healing spring. It had become their custom to repair to the baths for purification and cleansing. They offered up any malady or woundedness to the powerful mineral waters.

For several years, whenever the group gathered, a ritual had taken place. As the women first assembled, a candle was lighted and a small statue placed in its light. It was a figure of a woman, wrought in brass and bronze, her hair a twisted braid of burnished copper down her back.

The statue had been found at the bottom of a chest brought back from India by the missionary great-uncle of one of the women. In the circle cast by the candle, the presence of the statue drew the women back in time . . . to a time, long ago, when the earth was still held sacred . . . to a way of being with the earth and their own Feminine nature that the women had not lived out, but dimly sensed within themselves, waiting to be reborn.

The women gathered throughout the year in several different places. There was a concern that the statue would be damaged in travel. A small, silken bag was sewn to protect it, and another, of a sturdier fabric, as covering for the first. Eventually, a third was added. The statue was well protected.

At the opening of each retreat, the yarn holding the bags closed was slowly untied and the statue carefully placed at the center of the circle. Every springtime, the woman who led the group gave each woman a gift to help keep the power of the ritual alive within her throughout the coming year.

The small cloth bags given that springtime as remembrances of the ritual were replicas of the bags holding the statue. The gifts were placed on the pillows at night while the women slept. The first woman to awaken and open her gift came in quietly to say her thanks for her "first and only Goddess bag." She wondered aloud how she would fill it. The name seemed fitting, and the gifts were remembered as the Goddess bags.

Later that same morning, the women sat on a terrace looking out over the woods. They spoke of the meaning, for each of them, of receiving the empty bag. What would each woman place into it from her own uniqueness and life?

A woman prepared to speak, brushed a strand of dark hair from her face:

"I offer into this silken bag the whole of my life as woman . . . joy and suffering both . . . all that is sacred to me: the smooth, flat stone from the day on the beach when my husband last told me he loved me, a few days before he died . . . The old damask napkin from the day I took tea with my great-grandmother, when she was ninety-two . . . Two dried flowers, the red, from the day my first daughter was born, and the lavender, from the day I thought I would die from the pain of her death."

The woman bowed her head. The women sat in silence around her, as witness to her pain.

The youngest woman spoke, her chestnut hair aglow in the soft spring light:

"Suddenly, I see the depth of the woundedness in my woman-hood. I would not have thought, before, of honouring our sorrows or valuing our wounds . . . of holding anything of the Feminine sacred. I realize that those of us so wounded will suffer the gravest doubts in placing anything of ourselves into the silken bag.

"I offer into it the wounding in my Masculine side. My fears, when I was young, that I could not achieve in the world. And, later, an opposite wound, as my life was devoured by work. Into this silken bag, I offer the one-sided judgement that keeps me, even now, from re-specting my own suffering, that fills me, instead, with shame for ever having suffered . . . shame, failure, and condemnation for having done my whole life wrong."

A slender woman listened thoughtfully, hand on her grey-blonde hair:

"I pray that we offer up our habitual denigration of our own Feminine nature . . . the denigration of ourselves that leaves us unable or unwilling to endure suffering, even the suffering necessary to discover our own souls.

"I offer up the impatience that makes us try to rip forth full-blown the answers to our lives, rather than trusting them to bring themselves forth from the Self in their own time. I offer this up and pray that a sense of quiet forbearance may be returned to us all."

The sun was low in the sky. The wind blew softly through the nearby trees.

The oldest woman began to speak, fell silent . . . sighed:

"I didn't expect to live so long, to see such change before I died. Into this silken bag I offer a wounding of great poignancy that I see in woman after woman: a pushing and pressing at ourselves, a coldness towards our own pain . . . an expectation of ourselves to be invulnerable.

"I feel a deep concern for the lack of human kindness that I see among us . . . for an attitude that meets suffering from a safe, crisp platform of solutions rather than witnessing its truth from within our own experience of pain."

The slanting rays of the setting sun shone on her silver hair.

"Into this silken bag, I offer all that has been most scorned of the Archetypal Feminine realm . . . that it may be redeemed and healed and become most sacred to us all."

I listen in wonder
         . . . spring returns.

How might your life have been different if you remembered sitting with your mother, one day, when you were just a little girl . . . when an old woman spoke to you of listening to the wind and thinking of the lives of women . . . of the past, how far our grandmothers came, of the future, open before us.

If the old woman had taken out a soft old cloth and begun to sew . . . and said that she was making a small bag for you, to hold your understanding of the Feminine . . . that you must offer into it all that reflected your own image to yourself as daughter to the Great Mother. And then, words you did not understand until many years later, "Fill it from your conscious woundedness, from your deepest awareness as woman, and lastly, from your joy."

Then, if she had looked into your eyes and said very quietly . . . that as you made your offerings into the bag, the self-image of the Goddess, also, was being filled anew . . . "It is our sacred duty to offer into this bag all that will bring a new sense of the Feminine to heal and sustain us all."

How might your life be different?

I sit listening

as the wind

asks its eternal questions:

What will our generation of women

pass on to our daughters?

What will be our legacy

to the daughters

of our great-granddaughters?

And the earth

murmurs her response:

Answer yourself . . .

. . . yourself.

Her work
WITH THE MASCULINE WITHIN HER

Welcoming her energy

A May breeze murmurs from the meadow
. . . wafts of lilies-of-the-valley
. . . memories of spring commencements.

An image drifts to me:

A group of women of many ages gathers in the bright spring sunlight, young women in caps and gowns, their mothers and their teachers. A slender, blonde woman stands up, adjusts her doctoral robes . . . briefly touches the hands of the women next to her . . . looks at the young women seated around them:

"We mothers and teachers have asked you here, hoping to share our experience of our animus energy with you younger women. We are so proud of you! You have marshalled this wonderful energy so well to complete your studies, prepare for your professions!"

She nods to the black woman sitting nearest her, also in doctoral robes: *"We were remembering how it felt as our own Masculine energy first appeared: our lofty spiritual longings . . . our beautiful adolescent hero-worship of brilliant and beloved teachers . . . our sense of justice emerging . . . and our fearsome goal-directedness!"*

❖ ❖ ❖

As a young girl begins to grow up, the animus awakens within her. It brings bursting energies, a sense of power and purpose not present to her before. Now she must discipline this energy as she seeks to distinguish herself in academics, athletics, artistry: in all areas of achievement and accomplishment.

At this time, the daughter temporarily needs to separate from the mother to develop her animus powers. She must cut her roots from the Feminine ground and make a fearful crossing to the Masculine. During this crossing, the animus draws the girl as far away from the Feminine as she will ever be.

Now the girl needs a Masculine role model in the outer world for her newly-awakening animus. The encouragement from her father or male teachers is essential, especially if her mother has not worked with her own Masculine energy. The absence of this encouragement results in exaggerated feelings about the Masculine and an abstractedness that does not allow the girl to ground herself: a vacuum rather than a solidness in her feelings for herself as a woman.

"When women professionals of our age were growing up," the blonde woman continues, *"we identified with our fathers or male teachers. I didn't want anything to do with the diffuse Feminine ways of my mother or her friends."*

The black woman by her side interrupts laughingly: *"I'm sure that I was headstrongly anti-feminine as I identified with my Masculine side. I was enjoying its power, and I was strutting its stuff!"*

Then she smiles across the group at her own daughter in cap and gown: *"How lucky you young women are to have the understanding of mothers who went through these stages of development themselves.*

Welcoming her energy

"If the mother can remember that her daughter's struggle is against the entire Feminine realm, and not against her personally, she may be able to provide a container for the struggle that is broad enough that her daughter will not need to make a complete schism between them.

"By lending loving support, the mother may be allowed to serve as mentor for this new energy . . . may provide compass, charts, and sea anchor for her daughter's maiden voyage through these troubled and murky waters . . . May be allowed, to guide what may finally emerge as radiant qualities of leadership and excellence in her daughter's adult womanhood.

"But if the mother is unclear in her own relationship with her animus, unable to develop her talents or to find her voice, the situation will be painful for all. The Masculine energy will act out in chaotic disruption of the relationship, as mother and daughter are locked in a power struggle, turning household peace into a shambles. Mother will be unable to understand or tolerate the undirected energy in her daughter . . . will dig in her heels on the old issues of a clean room and a modest demeanour. And the girl will be scathing in her criticism of the mother."

Another woman interrupts, visibly upset: *"If only there had been someone to help my mother and me! We were terrible to each other. I needed her love, and I think she needed mine. How I wish there had been someone to give us some understanding of what was going on!"*

The black woman nods sympathetically: *"I'm so sorry for the pain that you both suffered! If only there had been someone to help your mother see that it was temporarily your task to overthrow all of her values. The mother may be the only one with steadiness enough to help the girl gain some clarity with her obstreperous young animus.*

"If the father tries to deal with this unruly side of the daughter, he may lock into combat with it, competing and needing to conquer it, and trying to break the girl's spirit. But the mother may realize that the more spirited the girl is at this age, the more glowing her leadership abilities may be when she is fully mature.

"A mother must know, in her heart, that she represents the very ground of womanhood to which her daughter will later return, this time no longer grafted onto and sustained by the roots of the mother, but striking root, herself, in the ancient Feminine ground."

The woman pauses in thought . . . then slowly reaches out to touch the lilac by her side: *"I marvel when I remember how wonderfully my mother handled this stage of my growing up. She fostered the relationship between my father and me, made the natural attraction between us feel safe, and helped him provide a good role model for the Masculine side of me. She encouraged Father to listen to me, to help me draw my thoughts together, sometimes even to help me take a stance!*

"My mother must have known how a girl's whole sense of herself can be affected by criticism, especially if it is stinging or harsh, how the animus will pick it up and undermine her with it for years to come. For she listened so caringly to my pain."

Two women stand to respond. The first speaks:

"My father and brothers saw me as competition . . . a poor second to father, fair game to all those brothers. And my mother saw me as a threat . . . and put me out of her kitchen and study. I had no one to support me . . . no encouragement from any direction.

"I became as tough as my brothers . . . merciless to myself. My inner voice is still as nasty to me as they were. To this day, I can feel that pain and rebelliousness, as if I can't do anything anyhow, so why try? I am learning, only now, to marshall my energies and abilities in a way that gives meaning to my life. And I'm scared for the time my three little girls will need me to befriend, in them, what was never befriended in me."

The second woman speaks:

"I am so very grateful. Something quite different happened to me. A professor acknowledged me in class as I sat amidst my peers. I had presented a short paper on Aeschylus. When I finished reading, the professor looked straight at me and said, 'Miss_____ , you have a keen and subtle mind.' He was a wonderful model for the Masculine side of myself. That happened nearly forty years ago and still helps me feel secure about my skills."

A white-haired woman walks slowly into the group. She had lingered at a Grandmothers' Tea held earlier, across the meadow:

"We oldest women are so moved at what lies before you younger ones. In our time, it was taken for granted that much of a woman's development would be lived out through a man. There were stories told humorously of "my son, the doctor" when sons or husbands fulfilled what the woman was not allowed to do.

"But now, you are developing your own talents and bringing all of your gifts to flower. We oldest women want you to know that we believe in you . . . that you have the opportunities and responsibilities that can change the world!

"We send our encouragement for success in that outer realm. And we send our warmest blessing that your young woman's spirits will be nourished by striking deep roots in the inner realm of the Feminine.

"For somehow . . . somehow . . . "

. . . the breeze wafts an almost unfathomable fragrance of lily-of-the-valley as the old woman takes the hand of the slender black woman in doctoral robes, drawing the gathering into a circle:

" . . . somehow," she continued, *"we old ones want you to know of a vision we have seen only dimly. Of a nobility and power and wisdom that lies within all women, but sometimes is not lived out.*

"You all know that your mothers will always be here in a circle around you as you work with your gifts. And we oldest women promise that we will be here, also, in an outer circle, holding in our hearts that ancient vision of women . . . praying that it will come alive . . . watering the roots of all of us in the Feminine ground."

The woman who had begun the morning stood up, tears sparkling in her eyes:

"And when the time comes for each of you to lovingly help your own daughter welcome her new energy, let her know that we feel her excitement, that we respect her struggle . . . that we have struggled, too.

"And that there is a place for her here with us, rooted in the ground of the Feminine!"

How might your life have been different if, once when you were a young girl . . . worried about your studies and still wanting to be helpful at home . . . your mother had quietly looked at you, one evening, and said, "It's all right, dear, I'll clear the table tonight. I know that you have a test tomorrow. Go, do what you need to prepare . . . and take a little time for yourself."

And then, if she had said, very softly, with a smile,
        " . . . later, let's look at the moon together
            . . . there's a lovely spring breeze blowing."

How might your life be different?

Embracing her encounter

I sit listening to the wind
. . . wondering and worrying
about our work with the animus.

Sometimes the Masculine side of us seems just like the men in a woman's life: she cannot get along with them and she cannot get along without them. Until she becomes aware of the Masculine energy within and consciously engages with it, it remains an autonomous force, out of her control. It keeps a woman focused on what happens around her, rather than on developing herself as deeply as she can.

The complete absence of animus energy would leave a deathly stillness . . . the woman would have no power to become who she truly could be!

There is a strong connection between a woman's animus and the men around her, like two mirrors facing each other, one inside and one outside the woman. When a woman first works to develop herself, both mirrors may seem unsympathetic. But as she grows, she will see her growth reflected in both inner and outer mirrors. As the Masculine within begins to help her express herself, the men around her begin to listen. And as she dares to speak out to the men in her daily life, the Masculine figures in her dreams reflect their growing respect.

Years ago, a group of women met to discuss this energy. We knew it was affecting our relationships with the men in our lives, and we wanted to know how to work with it. But we had no idea how to begin. And we were tired of worrying!

One woman told her own story of encountering this energy. But soon the discussion became generalized and full of puffy abstractions. By the end of the afternoon, we disbanded in disarray, taken over by the very side of ourselves we had been trying to discuss . . . As if it did not want to be exposed and have its power threatened!

How were we ever going to engage with this energy, and not just be blown about by it?

We decided to try again and stay with only our subjective sharing. A hearty woman began:

"I was raised quite traditionally. We knew nothing of women developing themselves. We identified completely with patriarchal views, expressed all the accepted attitudes. On good days, everything seemed rosy for us: nice little women staying in our places. And frighteningly unaware of our own existence as women!

"But on bad days, and in a black mood, I stood at the kitchen sink, dish cloth idly in hand, or stared listlessly over the copy machine out of my office window. The animus burst into my dreams as an intruder breaking in at the door. And it burst just as impulsively into my daily life . . . tearing at the garden, pounding at my typewriter, or scolding at my husband. And it was I who was doing it!

"I saw the same harsh qualities in every man I met, without realizing that those were the qualities of my untamed animus. It was blowing undirected and devastating all in its path. And as I tried to confront it, it called out heavy artillery. I was assailed by criticism from within and without. On the outside, from men who were actually judgemental as well as from those who were kinder. And on the inside, stinging rejection from all my old inner judges. It was a terrible time!"

She covered her face with her hands. The woman nearest her silently rested her hand on the woman's shoulder. A yellowed newspaper clipping fell from her journal onto the floor. She picked it up as she spoke:

"I cut this out many years ago and labeled it "The Energy of the Animus United Against the Woman as She Begins Her Encounter Within." It is a frightening picture. Nine or ten men in a close cadre, standing on the steps of the Supreme Court . . . their faces full of accusation and twisted into snarls. The picture reflected exactly the Masculine energy within me as it projected out and was reflected back by the men around me. So full of insults and judgement, as I began my inner work!"

A very young woman broke in:

"I'm finally figuring it out! If the men around us do not treat us with respect, then the men in our dreams treat us disrespectfully, too, and we feel badly about ourselves. Last week, I took a big risk and asked the man at the desk next to mine to pick up his share of the work. That night I dreamed of a man helping me carry a burden. But this surely was not how to begin!"

An older woman laughed and reached out to touch the younger woman's hand: *"We begin however we can! None of us really knows how. I began to encounter the animus at a time when I was very critical of myself and others. I knew something was at me and I had to communicate with it.*

"So, in an image, I summoned all of the male figures from my dreams. Then I wondered if I could be less imperious. If I could not only encounter those figures but also embrace the encounter with warmth! So I invited them to a council as ambassadors and couriers. Even set out colourful banners and flags to mark their seats.

Embracing her encounter

"One by one, I encountered each of those threatening figures who had judged me so harshly in my dreams. With dignity and formality, I told them that they must change. It was my life as a woman that was to be lived and their cooperation was needed. Then I asked the more encouraging figures, helpful teachers and mentors from the past, to take the others in hand. I asked them to be like knights preparing the young squires, teaching them how to serve with devotion and honour, and charging them with a trust to be my protectors and aides. Then I embraced each one of them and offered my heartfelt thanks."

The women sat quietly for a few moments.

Gradually, we realized how different this had been from our discussion the day before. We felt a keen appreciation for the women who had spoken. Because of their efforts to embrace their own encounter within, each of us was starting to understand how to begin the encounter within ourselves. We sat in silence together for a very long time. And we knew that their stories would stay with us.

❖ ❖ ❖

Slowly over the years, a woman's awareness of herself deepens as, again and again, she encounters the Masculine within. Now she can ask it to cease its judgement. She can call upon its strengths.

Finally it is available to help her develop herself!

How might your life have been different . . . if there had been a place for you to go, when you were a young girl, and had a great new energy that made you feel strong and sure of yourself, but sometimes made trouble with everyone around you . . . and something inside made you blame yourself for it all?

If there had been a place for you to be received . . . to just be, for a little while, with women who understood. If the women had listened and not blamed you . . . but had heard what you were going through . . . and they had been able to explain your new energy to you, and why it sometimes got you in trouble . . . explained it so clearly that you understood it yourself.

And you felt warmed by the support of those women . . . and relieved to finally know what had made all the trouble in the past. And then, if the women had told you that whenever you couldn't make sense of what was happening . . . they would be there to help . . . and you knew you could trust them.

How might your life be different?

Bringing forth her feeling values

The wind blows so insistently
I cannot hear the earth
erupting underneath.
Cut off, I listen
. . . listen.

The feeling values of the Feminine are woman's earth and blood. They form the foundation of human interaction and flow out to nourish all of society. In places where Feminine feeling values are ignored or persecuted, life itself becomes oppressive and barren.

In traditional patriarchal societies, where women have been kept dependent and must rely on "being taken care of," there is a lack of the clarity, incisiveness, and subtlety of mature and developed Feminine feeling values. What is allowed to be expressed by women in those societies is often merely an insubstantial and sweet applauding of the accepted standards established by the Masculine. Woman becomes a servant of these collective values.

A woman speaks: *"Even though my origins were very traditional, I managed to get an education, in spite of the attitudes against it. Yet I held an image of a woman, so frustrated and fatigued, that she could only lean her forehead against the doorframe, mute and tearless. There was no place for her inside or out.*

"Somehow, I did find a job within the given structure that seemed to offer survival, though little personal space. I called it my 'Cleft in the Rock.' But when I dreamed of a woman's body crushed amidst a rock pile, I knew that those were the rocks of that bloodless,

impersonal system that would never make room for me . . . would never make room for anything from the Feminine realm."

When a woman uses her energy only to reinforce what is outside of herself, she becomes cut off from her depths. Her own feelings and life values become inaccessible to her. She molds herself to external standards and loses touch with her individuality. She is cut off from all that is uniquely her own that could nourish her and those around her, cut off from the creative new answers so badly needed in the world today.

Cut off from her deeper sense of life, from the wisdom of her own unconscious, she lives in an arid approvable way. And her depths become enraged! The whole wellspring of womanly creativity within her is furious for not being tapped. And the greater the individuality and insight that have been dammed up, the greater the rage!

A woman speaks: *"My grandmother, my mother, and me . . . only allowed to smile and agree. Only allowed to affirm what was initiated around us, never allowed ourselves to initiate.*

"If grandmother tried to disagree, she became hysterical. And mother swung between hysteria and an opinionated animus, with no grounded Feminine ego between them. She was enraged that the men could never hear what she was unable to say.

"All those generations of women in my lineage using our energy in service to a system that had so little tolerance for Feminine feelings and values. Caught amidst all of this, I was depressed and cut off from myself, with no energy for the causes I had believed in only half a year before. Then my judging animus did its foul double-play, first damning me for my depression, then blaming me for having served so long what had not served me."

Bringing forth her feeling values

When a woman's animus joins with the Masculine surrounding to keep her Feminine values undeveloped, silent, and oppressed, there is no way that what is held within can flow. The woman becomes depressed. For what is within must flow out, her feelings and life values, all that the woman cares about and knows, most deeply to be true.

There is an old text, hidden away for centuries, that speaks of this:

> *If you bring forth what is within*
> *What you bring forth will heal you.*
> *If you do not bring forth what is within*
> *What is forbidden to come forth will devour you.*

And in a more ancient flowing out, women, during their menses, knelt on the earth each springtime to offer the gift of their own blood, certain that what they offered could bring the earth Herself to fullness and abundance again!

What if we women, in a symbolic way, offered our blood again, trusting that life itself would pour forth blessings in response? What if we might offer our life-blood in working to replenish our society with the Feminine values that have been so cut off . . . values of devotion to the earth and matter and to the individual . . . the values of the deeper Self?

What if we began to trust our feelings, even our depression, as our deepest truth? Began to respect our rage, being careful not to identify with it; but to honour it as holding within itself all the ancient Feminine, so long dormant, neglected . . . forbidden for so long to come forth.

What if we women began to stand by our pain, and refuse to let the animus invalidate it . . .

To shriek it in wordless, guttural cries,
paeans of despair to the gods:
The anguish of suppressed feeling values
of our mothers and their mothers before them,
of lost devotion to matter,
lost Feminine sovereignty,
of rain forests felled,
water spilt with oil,
...the anguish of the earth herself!

Imagine the significance if we women could heal the split between our developed animus and our unlistened-to womanly values. The significance if each woman among us would be willing to consciously suffer her own share of the anguish that says something is vastly wrong in the values of this world today.

Imagine the significance if every woman would be willing to bear the pain and isolation that must be endured, each time, to bring our values to expression. Imagine the significance, if each one of us would pour out her devotion, as our ancient sisters poured out their blood. Pour out our passion and devotion and await the response . . . as the ancient Feminine Archetype brings forth her values anew!

How might your life have been different, if, as young woman, there had been a place for you to go when you felt overwhelmed by the power of your feelings? If you had been received by women older than yourself . . . and helped to witness your feelings . . . and to trust their truth.

If the women had made a place for you by the fire and let you share your feelings . . . your pain and anguish and hurt . . . even your wordless rage.

And, as the fire burned low, you looked into the glowing embers . . . and knew how different it would have been for your mother and grandmother before you . . . if they, too, had been received by women when they needed to be heard. If women, then, could have helped them trust that their feelings served a purpose . . . that women's feelings might bring truth to bear where it was needed.

How might the lives of all of us be different?

Honouring her intuition

The wind blows clouds across
the strange, dark face of the moon
. . . hardly there at all
against the last piercing rays of the sun.

The element of the Feminine most difficult to comprehend is the lunar spirituality of her Feminine intuition ... the strange, ineffable quality of the dark face of the moon.

A woman's drawing showed this: one delicate, dark line on an otherwise empty page . . . a woman's face in profile, one tear falling on her cheek. The woman named it *The Nothing Against the Something*, this ephemeral lunar quality of woman's intuition . . . elusive, mute, and weeping . . . impossible to articulate.

For the intuition offers itself in glimpses hardly seen. Modern society, unfortunately, places little value on "things unseen." And the more distinctly Feminine a woman's intuition, the more it lingers in shadow beside the brightness of her inner Masculine. The subtler her intuitive gift, the greater her struggle to bring it forth. The animus will make it seem hardly there at all.

Woman's intuition is easily dismissed by the rational Masculine mind, as well as by the woman's animus. If older women around her have not learned to work with their own intuitive process, they cannot help the intuitive woman trust in her gift. She is caught between two aspects of the animus.

On one side, a judging patriarch invalidates her subjective perceptions. He values already established belief systems in the society around her that make no room for her uniquely personal new revelations. This judging patriarch animus undermines any intuitive awareness she has, pointing out achievements of others in more visible realms. She will feel that her intuitive gifts are nebulous and insubstantial.

The woman's animus projects itself out onto others and seems to come at her as disregard from those around her. She somehow becomes entangled in groups that do not recognize or value her gift. And the more vibrantly her vision presses to emerge, the more vehemently the inner patriarch thunders: She feels condemned it she dares to speak her truth.

The second aspect of the woman's animus is an immature Peter Pan. Sometimes pouty and irritable, he refuses to grow up and help the woman take herself seriously. He makes her see her own gifts in others, rather than in herself, inhibits her from developing them in a responsible way to challenge the established order. Then he engages in a frenzy of activity to distract her from bringing them forth.

Dapper and debonair, the Peter Pan animus runs the woman all over to lectures and workshops, keeping her an admiring disciple of the vision she thinks is in others, seeking from them the depths she cannot own within. Finally, he drops her at her doorstop, empty and depressed.

Caught between these two aspects of the animus, the woman is in terrible pain. For the intuition may be her strongest inherently subjective Feminine component. When she cannot own these depths, she is left hollow, robbed of her essence. The truest voice within her seems condemned by those around her, yet is so unclear inside her that she cannot bring it forth.

If only the intuitive woman could realize how deeply her gift is needed! For her intuition is the living connection, the conduit to the Self. Through this conduit flows the essence of life that keeps the soul of humanity alive!

When a society is not nourished by a connection to the deeper Self, it can easily be taken over. Oppressive mass belief systems appear that lead to barrenness and spiritual sterility. And the more oppressive the system around her, the more the woman's intuition will struggle to emerge. She may feel that she will die unless she can bring it forth.

At this point, no matter how painful or frightening, the woman must realize her position as visionary in the society around her. What she intuits may be the thimble-full of truth that only she can perceive, the vital new message that can overcome the stagnation of the established order.

Now the woman must have the courage to work with her vision, no matter how fragmentary it may seem. She must challenge the crushing oppression from the judging patriarchs within and around her, all that condemns her to silence, and demand of the immature Peter Pan that he help bring her vision to words. She must trust the truth of what is there, inside, and finally let go of worrying how it will be received.

Now the moment has come for the woman to own her maturity and authority. She must feel her compassion for her society, know her special place within it, as an intuitive, and take her stance. At this moment, she must speak, even if her voice trembles or her whole body shakes. Let it strengthen her to remember the ancient Feminine seers who wept as their vision poured through them, and the Quakers, who trusted the shaking as a sign of truth being revealed. Finally, the woman must reach down inside her and out to those around her, as she lets flow what has been locked inside!

A group of women gathered to hold their concerns in the light. The woman who spoke into the silence was a poet and artist: *"My animus reflected so clearly the men in my family history, men of power in the world, who thought women were charming, but of little consequence beyond that."*

The woman's father, a general, could not understand the pain it caused her mother when he was called to war. He had no comprehension of a deeper Feminine nature, no tolerance for darkness or suffering in any form whatever. Against this wall of judging patriarchy, the deep well of her mother's feeling and intuition was unacknowledged and unexpressed. Her mother's suffering, so rejected at the level of consciousness, dropped through to the cellular level: she was diagnosed with cancer.

The daughter continued, *"Two decades later, I fought cancer, also. My mother's illness had left a terrible void. For as mother tried to live up to my Father's values that denied illness or darkness, she simply disappeared into the hospital, without telling anyone, when her suffering became acute. Later, as I fought my own illness, I had terrible attacks of panic that I would disappear, too, without leaving a trace, unless I could express what I held locked inside."*

The woman's very rational animus dismissed her intuitive gifts, although her own rational development had earned a degree at Harvard. She studied comparative religion, the spiritual vision of others, yet could not take her own vision seriously. The bitter struggle of her intuitive nature could be expressed only in her art. *"I could only paint my anguish, the terrible struggle of my deepest Feminine nature so rejected by my animus.*

"Only after years of suffering did a symbol of transformation appear . . . the painting of a black saviour, the Masculine who knew my suffering. Knew the struggle to embrace one's inner truth in the face of the condemning establishment . . . The Nothing Against the Something *so deep in the Feminine vision.*

"Finally I could believe in my struggle and the truth that had been locked inside!"

How might your life have been different if, when you were a young woman, uncertain about something within, there had been a place where you could be with older women? . . . And if, as you simply sat with those women, you knew, somehow, that they knew about uncertainty themselves.

If, one by one, each woman had spoken into the silence, of woman's intuition, of her sensitivity to life . . . and of the pain her sensitivity might bring. And the women had spoken quietly, of the strength they knew was needed for a woman to choose to stay vulnerable to her own sensitivity.

And, that day, as you listened in the silence . . . you sensed the intensity and power in those women . . . and felt grateful that they had chosen to stay faithful to the truth within themselves.

How might your life be different?

Distinguishing her life

The wind drops.
The fragrance of fresh-mown hay
drifts across the fields
. . . the first harvest of late summer.

I sit listening . . . remembering a woman whose life was rich in harvest. Supervisor in a large state hospital, she was retiring, after years of service, with recognition and honours. She received official citations . . . and a cat to keep her company.

Things seemed to be going smoothly. She redirected her energy from the hospital to her private practice . . . and, of course, tended the cat. Oh, perhaps she was working a bit more than she wished, she said, *"but things would even out."*

And, yet, the situation seemed to shift the other way!

Years before, she had known that her father, a man of the open plains, was terribly proud of his daughter . . . his sons came ten years later . . . and he worked to develop the skills and bravery of his golden-haired little girl. The story she remembered most poignantly, told with pride and pain, was of the day she had circled the house, at her father's command, to test her endurance and courage . . . barefoot in the snow.

As the girl grew, she went on to discipline herself in many different directions:

"I always did well in school. Like many women of my age, I was taught to use the mind in a purely rational way . . . as if life could be understood logically. But I had no understanding or tolerance for my own needs for nurture or rest. That inner driving force allowed

me as little softness as my father had. During the years of my marriage, I had my husband install light bulbs in the garden and weeded far into the night.

"I have mourned so long the difficulty I have had in relating to women. As a young girl, my feeling needs were left unsupported. Mother took pride in my mind and accomplishments, but she related very little to the rest of my development. There was a deep well of undifferentiated feeling within me, full of isolation and pain, that was never recognized by her.

"In my adolescence, I was perplexed as Mother set me the task of accomplishing her goals, while she sat chatting cozily with my more girlish girlfriends. No wonder that, years later, I was fearful of betrayal by women. As much as I longed for their closeness, I felt too alienated from the Feminine to allow myself to be received.

"With my children, also, there was difficulty. I knew they respected my abilities, for they both followed in my professional footsteps. Yet they spoke of me as an island of unrest, offering nowhere to dock, whenever they expressed concern about my personal well-being. After all, I had trained myself to manage with so little regard from others . . . the girl who ran barefoot in the snow!

"The very efficiency and capability that had always served me so well, was, of course, my undoing . . . my quiet time always stolen, since I was so able to cope. Stopped in the hospital corridors by every troubled face, on the way to every meeting . . . and always arriving late. I was at war with time, plain old Chronos time . . . I had no idea at all of what Kairos time was about.

"And then, one day, the cat ran away.

"Bereft, I knew I had to bring my life back to myself. I realized that the formality of the name I had chosen for 'Mr. Cat' reflected my reluctance to recognize my own simple creaturely needs.

"For the first time in my life, I became aware of the necessities of nurture and care . . . began to give consideration to food, took time to prepare it thoughtfully. I knew I must free myself from the compulsive false energy of an animus that knew no natural tiredness: I arranged for a series of vigorous massages . . . then for a second series, gentler than the first.

"I made a promise to myself to give time, each day, to my journal . . . dreamed of making the journey to hold my first grandchild in my arms . . . the daughter of my daughter.

"On the weekend, I walked by the river.

"I began to clear away the thousands of things I had saved, waiting for time to savour them. Beautiful dresses, now too small, that I never found occasion to wear, bought to give me a special feeling about myself as a woman. I folded them into a box and grieved for a side of myself that had never been allowed to live.

"The books were the hardest to sort. I had always thrived on reading and the world of ideas. But I knew I would never have time to uncover my own ideas of life if I were to read every one of those carefully-hoarded words.

"I sorted a lifetime of papers.

"And now I am sorting out the way I learned to use my mind, devoid of womanly knowing. The young women of my generation were taught to shunt aside feelings, the Feminine subjectivity that is our very earth and grounding. It has taken me years to recover from the *barrenness of my life . . . to finally embrace my truth, rather than to reject it.*

"A few months ago, I heard the expression 'A Woman, Distinguishing Her Life.' I loved the two meanings it had for me: to graduate or retire with honours, distinguishing herself in that way. But also, to sort and delineate, as I have had to do, so that I could begin to see what really belonged in my life . . . distinguishing the content and meaning of my life from everything surrounding it . . . to allow the essence of my own individual life, at last, to emerge.

"Towards the end of the summer, late one afternoon, something happened that told me I was finding my thread. One of my women graduate students came by for a conference. We sat, for a while, towards sunset, discussing her paper and ideas, the caring we both felt for her work.

"Then she read me her first paragraph: 'I am exploring how the Feminine thinking function might differ from the Masculine's, how we might incorporate our new consciousness of ourselves as women with our inner Masculine side. Imagine what might happen in the next few generations if we approach our thinking with a separate womanly awareness: embrace our Feminine feeling values as the very warp of our process . . . shuttle between mind and heart to weave a wondrous, whole new fabric!'

"She put down her thesis and looked at me with tears, 'Thank you for your heart-mind.' "

*A fine light breeze rustles the leaves
against the darkening sky.
The tiniest star
sits twinkling on the horizon.*

How might your life have been different if, late one afternoon, near the end of the summer, as you thought of the opening of school . . . of trying, again, to learn to use your mind in traditional ways . . . something wondrous had happened?

If the women who were your teachers had invited their young women students . . . even the littlest girls . . . to come to sit in a circle . . . and, of course, you sat there, too? And you sensed the excitement in the voices of those women teachers as they spoke of a different way to use your fine, young minds.

If you sat and took a deep breath and felt the wonder of it all . . . the wonder of women sitting in a circle, under the open sky, just outside the school . . . women gathered to share their wisdom with the young women in their care. And you knew, from that day forward, that nothing would be quite the same . . .

How might your life be different?

I sit listening

as the wind

asks its eternal questions:

What will our generation of women

pass on to our daughters?

What will be our legacy

to the daughters

of our great-granddaughters?

And the earth

sings her response:

Offer yourself . . .

. . . yourself.

Her return
TO FEMININE GROUND

Her contagion

I sit listening
the wind blows . . .

As a woman matures, she deepens in her knowledge of her work within . . . moves toward a closer relationship with the Self. She has worked diligently to find her inner direction, struggled to free herself from slavishly following the directions of the animus.

Yet, sometimes, even at this stage, the animus exerts a counter-pull. A woman speaks: *"Once again, I feel endangered by the judging patriarch inside. It continuously keeps me concerned with how I appear to others. I suffer a mild contagion, as if I am running a slight fever and keep feeling I should do something important without knowing what it should be.*

"The animus pushes at me, makes me live from outside myself, flipping me back and forth from centeredness to over-dispersed activity, and keeping me unaware of the frenetic ambivalence or of how I betray myself. I try to do my work in time that does not exist. Never allow myself time to think or for my freshly washed hair to dry."

I cannot notice the sunlight
streaming in at the window
. . . the pungence
of the scarlet chrysanthemums
on her reading table.
I lose a sense of the realness and substance of my life.

❖ ❖ ❖

A group of women that I met with had a troubling experience. The women had wanted quiet time to reconnect with themselves and a chance to speak thoughtfully of their work to develop themselves. As the group drew into the silence, one woman seemed ill at ease. She began to speak at length, paragraphs of outer detail, without telling her own feelings about anything. Then she asked repeatedly if we had understood, knowing perhaps how remote she had been from her real Self.

As carefully and sensitively as we could, while still being honest with her, we told her that she had spoken for a long time. She claimed hurt beyond measure, accused us all of being uncaring and sarcastically insisted she thought this was a place for sharing. Although a whole group of women had given their all, it was nothing to her animus! When she did not return later, we realized sadly that the animus might need to run its course.

Then we tried to understand what had happened: When women sit in silence and one woman speaks from her heart, the rest of us hear her deeply and all of us are nourished by the feelings and thoughts in our midst. The animus, threatened and fearing it will lose us from its control, becomes very active. A woman's dream tells us about this: *"A figure in a long grey robe welcomed women into a grotto. It looked like the robes of an ancient priestess, in a place held sacred to the Feminine. To the women's shock, it was a man in the robe, with red high heels showing beneath his hairy legs."*

This is our Masculine side. It has us acting omniscient in the very realm of the Feminine where it has no footing at all, out-womaning other women simply to feed its power drive. It dismisses and wounds women around us with little jokes and patronizing stories.

The animus-contagion invalidates the inner authority of our intuition and feelings, so we quote outer authority at length . . . denies the very life-blood of womanly intuition and feeling that could re-vitalize the Feminine values so weakened in the world today.

If only it were possible to alert a woman friend when the animus-contagion takes her over. Yet to stay so grounded that our own animus won't be stirred into action by the infected side of her. The only ways I know to break the contagion's hold are to finally be willing to sit in the silence or to deeply weep.

It was late in the day. A small group of women gathered in silence. One woman spoke: *"My animus never let me make a real commitment to my life. Too many fiancés, too many jobs, and even too many friends. Last year, I was offered a position at a regional center for the arts. There would be permanence and solidity, if I could make a commitment. Sure enough, my old inner voice spoke immediately, 'But my dear, that surrounding will bore you. What's the harm in staying free?'*

"That evening, an image came to me of an old nun who had taught mime at the academy many years before. 'Hasn't that inner trickster stolen enough from you? What's the harm, indeed! He's stealing your life!'

" 'It is not enough to intellectually understand our patterns. We must grapple with them and change them, or deceive ourselves. You have a chance, now, to really lay a foundation for your life, an opportunity to make a contribution with something you truly believe in.' Her grey eyes softened for a moment as they looked into mine. 'Claim your dignity, and maturity and authority, and make a commitment to your deeper Self.'"

❖ ❖ ❖

The afternoon sun cast long shadows. There was silence to honour the woman's story. An older woman near her nodded quietly in understanding:

"Several years ago, I was invited to read my work in the town where I was born. I selected the material carefully, choosing passages that illustrated women's individuation, our movement away from outer conformity as we become ourselves.

"As the time drew near to return to my birthplace, I found myself frightened and shy . . . tempted to read, not passionately and full-heartedly as was my usual style, but like the schoolgirl those women had known fifty-five years before.

"The day before my journey, I was full of dreadful anxiety. Would I really present my own material in a sterile and 'proper' fashion? Betray this chance to witness to woman's individuation?

"When I entered the train the next day and tried to settle myself, a comforting image came . . . of a stately and beautiful actress in her role in Ibsen's Ghosts, which I had seen several seasons before. Her lines rang out, in my memory, of wishing to live a life of courage and vision, rather than to pass it in servitude to 'dead ideals and worn-out old beliefs.'

"As the waiter served coffee in the dining car, late in the afternoon, I selected the last material for my presentation. For the opening reading, I chose a poem in the voice of a mature woman:

"If I am so perpetually terrified
    of being called a bad girl,
so eternally blown about
    by the winds of my inner judges,
that I cling to any authority
    that grants me marginal approval,
then I risk that I might never, ever
    turn towards that within me
that guides and orders my existence,
    that lets the truth of my life emerge.

O! Grant me courage to become myself!"

The wind blows
    . . . leaves rustle, russet and gold.

Her contagion

How might your life have been different, once, long ago, when you had worked very hard to know what you knew inside, and were ready to bring it forth . . . but were suddenly filled with fear and guilt and unable to express yourself . . . and you felt utterly alone? If there had been a circle of women waiting to receive you, eager to listen to your understanding of life.

If the women had known, from their own lives, that whenever a woman dares to bring forth the deepest meaning from within, she will be attacked by an old force inside, whose only purpose is to keep things as they are . . . And the fact that those women existed made you feel less lonely.

And if the women had helped you, supported you with their warmth . . . and by the wisdom and daring of their lives, given you the courage to speak.

How might your life be different?

Her possession

The wind blows mysteriously
   . . . full of mesmerizing power.

As a woman works consciously with the Masculine side of herself, she learns its patterns and behaviours, begins to see, in the moment, how it influences her. Yet, even then, from time to time, she is snatched from behind . . . possessed.

The woman is the last to be aware. Her women friends or her husband are the first to feel the sting . . . and always, her poor children. All that is negative in the Feminine realm floods over the woman at this moment . . . the loathing of herself, neglect and abuse of the elemental . . . her body, family, and household! The door is open to cursing, to the nursing of old hurts, as the woman is taken over by this awesome negative power.

A woman tells her dream:

"I had been abducted and was being held captive in a room far above the earth . . . lured there by hypnotic praise.

I knew that my abductor was a terrifying destroyer of women and if I succumbed to his hypnotizing, I would become a destroyer, too!"

What can release a woman from this terrible spell? If a man tries to intervene, he may be attacked by the woman's rampaging Masculine side. For this side of a woman is only a brittle reflection of the warmth and strength of the true

Masculine and will try to destroy the outer man and dominate the situation.

Only if a man can remember not to be drawn into words, or into competition with the woman's animus, does he stand a chance of bringing her back to life.

Even her women friends face a risk from the destructive power. For when a woman is in the grips of animus possession, her true nature and feelings are inaccessible to her. She is unconscious of how hurtful her words and actions are. Only the deepest devotion from a woman friend might draw the woman back to her womanly relatedness. Through gentle nurture, the friend might be able to help the woman come back into the realm of matter, back to a wordless connection to her simple creaturely needs. By quietly attending her and expressing compassion for her pain, the friend might offer the most powerful healing of all: if the woman can weep, her tears will break the spell.

A woman spoke of the anguish brought by animus possession:

"I thought of myself as so spiritual that I was completely unconscious of my real behaviour. It was as if I were mesmerized, I rose so disdainfully above our daily life. The house was quite beneath me! I would not focus on a task. I cared so little for the material realm that I could not bring order to the matter of our lives.

"Every morning, my children went out like little disheveled ragamuffins, with everything all askew. And in the afternoon, when they returned from school, I would scream that they'd interrupted my meditation with their pedestrian concerns. While, to my evening study groups, I presented an opposite image: a self-conscious over-centeredness without any freshness or life.

"I blamed it all on my husband, who did not live up to my intellectual or spiritual ideals. He just went to work each day and came home to his workshop and garden. Thank God that, for the children, he was a warm and encouraging father.

"I don't know what rescued us all from that dreadful time in our lives. One day, I found myself thrusting my youngest child away as I prepared to lead my group. I knew something was terribly wrong.

"My little daughter's tears finally shocked me out of being possessed . . . brought me face to face with myself!"

There was silence as the women listening sensed the full danger in the woman's experience.

❖ ❖ ❖

The second woman waited, then began to speak:

"I carried all of the burdens during those painful years. Hardening my heart for so long let something else slip in the door. I can see it in the photographs taken of me during that time, the set of my jaw, the tilt of my head. My face became tough and cold.

"When I look back, at myself, it is with a deep compassion. I needed to have that toughness, then, but also to let it go. How impatient that harder side of me was with my womanly needs and hurt! I could not face the pain underneath or minister to it myself.

"Saddest of all was the loneliness. Women friends were driven away by my competitiveness, except for a very few who were as possessed as I. But I could not bear their cutoffness from feelings any more than they could bear mine. One by one, they all left.

Her possession

"Isolated and alone, I spent those terrible years hating men, most women, and, of course, myself. What finally broke the alienation was being held by a warm, silent man who refused to be drawn into words . . . simply held me closely until I started to cry. As my weeping deepened into sobs, I began to return to myself."

The three women sat in silence to honour the woman's words, then parted quietly to prepare a cup of tea.

❖ ❖ ❖

When the women came together again, they gathered close around the fire. The third woman began to speak:

"I was touched as you spoke of being silently held and return-ing to yourself. My experience was quite different. I was full of anger at my husband. He had said something that hurt me, and I held it to my heart.

"What could have been useful anger, if I had communicated it, became an entrenched rage. The insult became precious and exaggerated as I nursed my grievances and refused my husband's apologies. I shut myself into my study.

"I can see, now, the Masculine posturing in what I did, and how it cut me off from my husband's caring and honest concern. Even as my husband apologized, my animus convinced me that I was right, and I shoved my husband away. If only I had been able to let the flesh-and-blood man reach me, the inner imposter might have been ex-posed.

"One morning, I realized that I couldn't stop being nasty to my husband. I felt as miserable as he. Yet, I was caught in something per-verse that wouldn't let loose of either of us.

"Late that afternoon, a woman friend came by and took me briefly aside. She spoke with me so caringly and seemed to see my pain. Rather than drawing me into words, she simply reached out her hand and stroked my aching head. She must have known how desperately I had needed to cry, for I sobbed a long while after she wrapped my shoulders warmly in her sweater.

"She asked if I would come with her the next day for the mineral baths and massage that our town is known for, then spoke a few words to my husband that, somehow, he understood.

"In the few days after that, she came back several times. Together we scrubbed with a bucket of hot suds . . . the whole house, the walls, the floors.

"Then, as the last rays of the late afternoon sun bathed the room, we washed the windows in my study."

The wind blows lightly
    . . . leaves drift down.

Her possession

How might it have been different for you, when you were terribly upset and full of harsh self-judgement, if there had been a place where you could be received by a woman whom you trusted?

If the woman had listened in silence as you began to speak? And there had been a feeling of such simple acceptance from her that you were able to weep . . . finally, able to weep out all of the confusion and pain that you had held inside for so long . . .

And she wordlessly held your hand.

How might your life be different?

Her individuation

> I sit listening . . .
> The wind blows
> a woman's image to me.

Although the schedule had been pressing, I felt quite satisfied at a recent decision to take more time for myself . . . one-half hour a day, for walking or reflection.

Then, that night, I awoke and was transfixed by moonlight streaming in at the window . . . and at the image of a woman . . . scrawny and malnourished . . . her face covered with ashes . . . clothing torn by thorns.

"I am the neglected and crazy part of you . . . the holy part inside, which you so often deny . . . bustling between kitchen and studio, cheerful and productive.

> "Don't you see I am dying?
> When will you recognize me
> as the most precious part of yourself?
> When will you grant me sovereignty?
> When will you give me your soul?"

> I knelt and wept in the moonlight . . .
> . . . let my tears wash the ashes from her face.

❖ ❖ ❖

The years pass. A woman matures. Her work with her
Masculine side ripens . . . her contributions to the society
around her carefully brought to harvest. The Self calls insistently. She must finally hear and respond . . . or take the other
path of hardening her heart against the voice within calling her
to become herself.

A woman must be very clear, now, in her ongoing task.
As she negotiates the voyage from the societal towards the Self,
her entire experience is transformed. She can begin to reject the
inner patriarchal decrees from the past that judged her so mer-
cilessly . . . that made her see her own anguish as simply another indication of her inadequacy and shame.

With this transformation, a woman can accept feelings
inside herself that were forbidden to her before. She can accept,
newly, her failures, her lacks, her obsessions . . . even her occa-
sional craziness . . . as she holds in her awareness all the ways
she has suffered in striving to fulfill values that were not her
own.

At last a woman cradles in her arms the woundedness
of being herself. No longer casting it out as the impediment
that prevents her growth, she can embrace her woundedness as
the essence, the soul of her uniqueness . . . that which has en-
abled her to become herself.

With this final acceptance of her woundedness, a woman's perception of her own suffering undergoes a profound healing. What had been the source of greatest shame, that most loathed in herself, slowly reveals itself to her as the seed of her truest gift . . . her pearl of greatest price, grown from her gravest flaw. She is released into her wholeness.

Finally, as a woman matures, she gives up the expectation of reaching a point of bare adequacy and moving on from there. At last, she understands that her task is simply to accept her woundedness . . . and to walk ahead with courage and compassion . . . keeping faith with her own life.

This is her individuation.

A woman sat alone and considered her condition. She was an editor of scientific journals who had recovered from starvation in all aspects of her life:

"I began to feel the poignancy of my own wounding . . . the poignancy of those old patterns set up, so long ago, as a protection against further wounding, in my little child way.

"I said, once, to my counsellor many months ago, 'But my patterns are pathological,' and she replied, 'Then that is finally what makes all the going back into one's personal history worthwhile. To be able to see the original wounding with such pathos, that you at last can feel compassion for that terribly wounded little child who wanted so strongly to survive that she was willing to adopt extreme patterns.'

"From the moment I heard those words, I knew that I must trust that my uniqueness stemmed from my own kind of wounding . . . grew directly out of it, not divorced or split off from it. I knew, from that day forward, that one day I would be able to stop loathing my woundedness . . . and hold it in esteem."

A second woman spoke:

"My parents must have wanted a completely different child! If my talents could not win instant fame, I was scorned for even trying. I couldn't imagine taking the risk of becoming more myself. All I had ever experienced was humiliation and despair for revealing, in any way, who I really was.

"My animus reflected my parents' negating attitude. Years ago, I named my inner judges 'the shit boys.' Far from being supportive helpers in my efforts to develop, they were the eternal critics who scorned anything I brought forth from within myself.

"I learned quite skillfully, over the years, to use myself as mirror and mentor for the creativity of others. I have helped many wordless people express themselves in poems . . . helped those with no sense of identity tell the pathos of their lives in writing their autobiographies. I have watched the radiance of dance emerge from eighty- and ninety-year-old bodies as our troupe toured the countryside working with the elderly.

"I have had to realize, as my deepest truth, that I could help bring out their spirit, while mine was held captive within.

"I wish, now, to be present to what is real inside me, to the anguish and chaos and fear. No longer to dress it up in impeccable tutorial service to the gifts of others . . . further and further estranged from myself . . . feeding on anything to fill the hollow.

"There are poems unborn inside me, and, if I live long enough, I wish to bring them to birth. I wish to stand firm against the expectations of disgrace for daring to have something inside me of my very own.

"Most of all, I wish to stay close to the apprehension of being immediately shamed. For if I only rise above my fear, as I have so often done, there will be no one to witness my wretchedness and mortification . . . no one to attend my wounding . . . no one to allow it to begin its process of transformation and healing.

Her individuation

"I have finally acknowledged my wounding as the thing in all the world that is most truly mine . . . and that acknowledgement has allowed me to begin to be myself.

"I am able, at last, to witness my wounding
. . . and I am, at last, in peace."

The sky darkens towards the evening.

How might your life have been different if, once as you sat in the darkness, suffering the most piercing shame for simply being yourself . . . you had sensed a presence nearby, sitting quietly in the shadows attending you . . . a forgiving Feminine presence?

If you had felt such a flow of compassion from that ancient presence . . . that you could begin to accept your flaws, even your gravest faults? And, deeply comforted in the flow of that compassion . . . you were able, at last, to embrace your own woundedness . . .

How might your life be different?

Her return

I sit listening . . .
   the wind blows
      a woman's image to me:

"I have crossed a chasm . . . stand alone, now, in a chamber . . . carved of dark, rich crystals, glowing deep within the earth.

A distant call beckons me onward . . . to a still more glowing chamber . . . then to another, richer still . . . chamber opening unto chamber, each glows more darkly than the last.

I know that these are the chambers of a mansion that once belonged to my Mother . . .

And I know that the openings . . .
   chamber unto chamber . . .
      are the moments of my life."

Out of a woman's acceptance of her woundedness comes a quietness and sense of peace. The transformation of the Masculine energy within her, from negating to supporting, allows her to become herself. She redirects her efforts from the outer to the inner realm . . . finally makes the return to Archetypal Feminine ground with her roots in the guiding principles of the deeper Self.

❖ ❖ ❖

A woman speaks:

"I feel as if I am becoming who I was meant to be. After all the years of outer-directed energy, I am coming home to the Feminine . . . coming home to myself. I am allowing myself to become a mature woman in the truest and deepest sense.

"Sometimes, as I sit listening quietly within, it seems as if the very air in the house has been transformed. There is a hush of tranquillity, an attitude of devotion filling every room.

"I feel a sense of connection to the self that I have been at other times in my life . . . to the girl and maiden from the past, to the developed woman of adulthood . . . and to the older woman I know that I shall someday be.

"As I allow myself to mature, a clarity emerges, never there before. I seem to know more surely than I have ever known what is mine to do, what must be left undone. There is a growing strength within me . . . and I realize, that while life's difficulties do not disappear, my steadfastness holds firm.

"As I allow myself to mature, an awareness comes of a slender ribbon of energy, no longer robust, as in my youth. I learn to tend it carefully . . . avoid excess, exercise restraint. To use my strength ever more sacramentally, for I suffer more each time I use it in service to old distractions.

"As I allow myself to mature, I find that I must do things the old, slow ways . . . perform my work so quietly that some part of me can always be listening . . . listening for the deeper sense of my life. Those few brief moments each day, that 'closet' in time that, as a young woman, I set aside to listen, are no longer enough for me.

Her return

"What I could slip by with while I was still in service to the values of the society around me is likely to make me ill now, at the level of the Self. I sense that the greater quantity of my time is being required, now, to reflect at the window seat . . . to see the leaves drift down . . . watch the snow clouds gather.

"As I allow myself to mature, I see that if I depart from my center and am over-busy for too long, it may take many days of quietness for me to make the return. And in dry periods, when the Self seems not to be present, I know that my task is simply to wait. Now, the only task . . . in devotion and submission . . . is to wait upon the Self."

Slowly over the years, as a woman allows herself to mature, she sees that she must keep the physical realm so simple that each object in her household becomes translucent . . . revealing its meaning and spirit to her as she polishes it in her hands . . . that this is her testament of devotion, the loving redirection of her energy from outer to inner realm . . . and the holding and hallowing in her hands of the moments of life itself.

Alone on the barren rocks,
I listen to the wind . . .
It blows the ancient, raucous call
of distant wild geese.
I know I am coming home.

How might your life have been different if, through the years, you had felt that there would finally be time enough for you?

If, very early one morning . . . as you sat at the window seat and watched a silvery mist slowly rise from the meadow . . . you heard, far off in the distance, the call of the wild geese?

And you remembered the first time you had heard that cry, many years before . . . with a chill up the back of your neck. And that you had known, even then, that the haunting, primordial cry . . . was the call of the ancient Feminine returning.

How might your life be different?

Her legacy

> I sit listening . . .
>> the wind blows
>>> a child's song to me . . .

An old woman sits in the dusk, an unlighted candle on the table before her. She picks up a soft cloth, begins to polish the small statue in her hands, as she has done many times before. She polishes the statue of a woman . . . keeping vigil in the stillness . . . polishing her own sense of life.

She hums a children's song that she says is very old . . . then she begins to sing:

> " 'This is the way we sow our seed . . .
>> gather our grain . . .
>>> bake our bread . . .
> This is the way we tend our lives
>> so early in the morning.'

"I learned that song, and others like it, at an afternoon gathering for children and their mothers, many years ago. Songs that told of the ways of woman, long before I was born . . . still knowing that the spirit with which a task was fulfilled made a difference in the greater order . . . and let a rhythm and meaning emerge from every step of her work.

"Woman, long ago, still in touch with the mysteries of nature . . . singing to the grass and the wind . . . knowing that her song was heard. Pouring out her devotion, as she poured out her menstrual blood, back to the earth again."

The old woman sighs:

"*Ah, those young mothers, that afternoon, had lost touch with so much of that. I cannot forget their faces, so desperate and stricken, as they sang their choruses of the ancient circle dances there in the meadow with their children . . . cut off from any meaning that might have made their tasks alive.*

"*That generation of woman . . . cut off from roots in the earth . . . or from knowing how to replenish the earth with their own womanly flow. So much of their Feminine energies blocked within them, like their milk, in those decades when women heeded the advice to schedule and bottle-feed their young.*

"*I sang a lament, that afternoon in the meadow, that a patri-archal way so pervaded . . . that woman no longer trusted her own in-stincts to nourish herself and her young.*

"*I sang a lament that women no longer encouraged an opening unto each moment that could allow it to unfold to the next . . . that they no longer let their own lives be alive and teach them how to live.*

"*I sang a lament that afternoon that the old ways of tending nature were dying. For I feared that, as they died, the life in our souls would die, too.*

"*I sang a lament, that afternoon in the meadow, for women of every age, overburdened and overworked, pressed between efforts for those they loved and the weight of their work in the world . . . with no time for rest or reflection on what their life was about.*"

The old woman pushes a strand of hair from her face:

"Ah, that was so long ago . . . so many ways were lost. I learned the songs as well as I could, so that someone might keep them alive.

"Once, as our circle of women came together a few years ago, I wakened, restless in the night . . . unable to go back to sleep. I sat for a long time on the terrace, wrapped in a woolen robe . . . watching the moon shine down on the wind-bared trees below.

"When I finally came back to the cottage, there was a glimmer of light from the kitchen. My old friend sat there, alone, by candle-light, the only one in the circle older than I. It was she who had taught the songs on the meadow that afternoon, long ago. She polished this little statue that night, telling me of her life . . . and mine.

"She left me her shawl when she died.

"She's gone now, but every year at this season, in the middle of the night, I sit, as she did, for so many years, polishing this statue . . . polishing, alone, while the younger women sleep."

The old woman puts down the statue, reaches for the matches to light the candle:

"That afternoon, long ago, I lamented. But as I sit polishing this statue, I know that a difference can be made as we women remember again to keep faith with our ancient ground . . . remember that the stillness at our center, as we sit in the glow of a candle, can help return a sense of order to the cosmos reflecting us.

"We lost touch for a little while, in the busyness of this world. But I know that a difference can be made if we women can remember that our blood and passion are needed . . . our fierce, tender love for the land. We can bring the cycles to wholeness again as we pour out our devotion . . . as we sing, once more, to the earth."

The old woman unfolds the shawl, wraps it around herself.

"We lost touch for a little while, in the noise and pain around us. But, I know that, for the children, a difference can be made if we can return to a sense of the ancient Maternal . . . return to the cradling embrace that offers solace and protection . . . that strengthens their sense of Self.

"We lost touch for a little while. But I know that, for the men around us, a difference can be made if we can remember a way of being that gives them a place to return, a Yin to receive their Yang warmth. A difference can be made as we help them learn to heal their own pain as well as ours . . . help them comfort their fears and affirm their heroic strivings."

The old woman smoothes the shawl . . . straightens her shoulders beneath it.

"The earth, the children, the men . . . they all need what was lost. But it is for our daughters . . . our daughters . . . that women must remember all that was left behind. It is our daughters who cannot go on with their lives unless we show them the way.

Her legacy

"It is for our daughters that we must rekindle the ancient ways of the Yin . . . help them hold the truth of their knowing deep within themselves and witness it with the full passion and power of their womanly being . . . help them to remember that the truth each woman holds within will come to realization not only through outer doing but through her inner holding.

"We lost touch for a little while, as we gained power over things seen . . . that woman's ancient chthonic power has to do with things unseen. For our daughters, we must return to the sacred Feminine ways of holding within our hearts our visions for their lives . . .

Of holding within,
  the essence and splendor
    of our daughters' possibilities.
      . . . the possibilities of all women
        . . . and dreaming them into being."

The old woman quietly picks up the statue and bends her head low to her task. As the candle flickers out, she sits in the darkness . . .

. . . polishing
  . . . polishing.

How might your life have been different if, one morning in the earliest springtime, something had drawn you to the woods? And in the cool mist, you had seen women of all ages, from every epoch in history, waiting in the stillness.

And you had knelt among them . . . had heard the trembling in the voices of the older women as they spoke of preparation, of individual sacrifice . . . of woman offering, out of her own uniqueness, her suffering, her devotion. And if, as you listened, you had a glimmer of hope that your work to develop yourself might make a tiny difference . . . help heal an ancient Archetype . . . restore a longed-for balance in the greater cosmos.

And you felt a sense of wonder, knowing that each woman kneeling there was considering inside herself what her offering would be . . .

How might your life be different?

I sit listening

as the wind

asks its eternal questions:

What will our generation of women

pass on to our daughters?

What will be our legacy

to the daughters

of our great-granddaughters?

And the earth

whispers her response:

Know yourself . . .

. . . yourself.

The Author

Judith Duerk

Judith Duerk was born in the Midwest and followed the call of her early love for music. She earned B.S. and M.S. degrees from The Juilliard School, studied as a postgraduate at the Mozarteum in Salzburg and at Indiana University, and taught at the university level before beginning preparatory work in the fields of psychotherapy and music therapy.

For many years, she has led groups of women on Retreat. She says, *"I am awed by the depth of healing that comes as women sit in a circle, by the power of women speaking one by one into the silence, and by the truth in their sharing. I am newly aware of the caring support that women offer each other and of the enormous difference it brings."* In addition to her daily work as a therapist, she is beginning the twenty-fifth year of teaching her classes in T'ai Chi.

Judith has noted that the sensitivity and strength of the men around a woman are helpful role models for her animus. Although her two sons are grown now, she recalls that *"when they were young, they liked to joke that all their mother cared about was Yin-Yang-Jung . . . but they really knew better."*

Her life has been deeply nurtured by the cycles of nature and seeking to care for them in return.

Deepening your Circle

Ideas to help draw your circle of women together:

Over the last ten years, in hundreds of women's circles around the country, women have gathered to study Judith Duerk's books. In a typical evening, one woman may read a single chapter aloud while the others sit listening, with their eyes closed. And then at the end, they may share their personal experiences or images—or perhaps memories from old dreams—that are evoked during the reading.

Your circle may want to reflect on the ending questions for each chapter, *"How might your life have been different if . . .?"* You may want to expand your reflection with the discussion questions offered here.

You may want to begin your circle the way Judith often begins her retreats: She asks the women to imagine that they are inviting the important women from their lives to join them, to sit just slightly behind them in the circle, all of the women from their whole life . . . those who were supportive and affirming, and perhaps those who might have been, but weren't . . . "the special woman teacher who reached out to you in second grade, the favorite auntie who always made you the lemon crisp cookies, the kindly neighbor lady who plucked the red tulip and gave it to you over the fence . . . and the woman professor or mentor who taught you so much." Consider your relationship with each of these women, positive and negative. Let them all be there surrounding you in your gathering of women.

Reading Group Suggestions
for *I SIT LISTENING TO THE WIND*

HER GROUNDING IN THE FEMININE

A *sense of time* (pages 20-25)

"For under the pressures of modern life, time has become compressed" (pages 23). How do you experience the compression of time? How might your life be different if you knew there would finally be enough time for you? Pages 21-22 describe "a shift in the experiencing of time." Has this kind of shift ever happened to you? What were your thoughts and feelings about this?

A *sense of identity* (pages 26-30)

The woman musician in this chapter "knew truly who she was and the value of what she gave . . . she did not make herself give more" (page 28). What are the signs that signal to you that a woman knows herself? What women mentors in your life seem to know who they truly are? What are some things you do or could do to recognize your own identity and worth?

A *sense of sustenance* (pages 31-36)

This chapter describes the choice between a "wire" mother and a "soft" mother. What is your experience of each? How might your life be different if you had a place among women where you knew you could always go for safety and comfort?

A sense of voice (pages 37-42)

Each woman in this chapter describes finding a way to speak in her own voice, to express herself in her own style. Think of a time when you felt no one understood you. How did you feel when you were unable to communicate what you knew you wanted to say? How might it have been different for you if supportive women had listened to you and encouraged you to let your true voice emerge?

A sense of sacredness (pages 43-47)

In this chapter Judith describes small, silken bags that each woman symbolically fills with something that is sacred to her. What container would you chose? As you picture this container, think of some fact, memory, or image from your life that you would like to place in its empty space. What feelings surface for you as you picture doing this?

HER WORK WITH THE MASCULINE WITHIN HER

Welcoming her energy (pages 52-58)

In this chapter, the women teachers speak about their experience of first meeting their animus/masculine energy. What are your memories of first meeting this energy within yourself? Do you remember "strife" between you and your mother at this time? Did anybody help you to welcome this energy in yourself? How would you like to help your daughter or niece welcome this energy in herself?

Embracing her encounter (pages 59-63)

"Slowly over the years, a woman's awareness of herself deepens as, again and again, she encounters the Masculine within" (page 62). What is your experience over the years of confronting your own inner masculine side? How has your relationship with this masculine energy changed over time? How have you been able to call upon its strengths rather than its judgement?

Bringing forth her feeling values (pages 64-68)

Five women in this chapter share their experiences of feeling cut off from themselves, from their creativity, from their feelings. What do you recognize in their stories that relates to you? How have you experienced this kind of pain? How might it be different for you if there were a place where you could go whenever you felt overwhelmed by your feelings?

Honouring her intuition (pages 69-74)

Judith writes that the intuition of woman is very hard to describe. How does your own intuition work? What does it do for you? Is it ever troublesome? What gifts does your intuition bring you?

Distinguishing her life (pages 75-79)

The woman in this chapter speaks of two different meanings for distinguishing her life: One is the more common definition of "earning honours," while the other is finding the meaning of one's individual life. In what ways have you seen your women friends or women leaders distinguish their lives in each of these ways? What are your own experiences of these different types of "distinguishing"?

HER RETURN TO FEMININE GROUND

Her contagion (pages 85-90)

This chapter describes the eruption of misunderstanding and ill will between women brought about by an "untamed animus." What is your own experience of this happening between women? How have you and the women around you been able to recover from this kind of competition or conflict? What do you find helps you keep from trying to "out-woman" other women?

Her possession (pages 91-96)

Possession by the animus is more gripping and lasts a good deal longer than the kind of contagion described in the previous chapter. It is much harder to break its hold. Have you ever had an experience like this or seen it with a woman friend or relative? In what ways did you, or the woman, become "swallowed up" by the episode, convinced that you were "right"? How might it have been different for you if there had been someplace where you could safely weep out all of the confusion and pain?

Her individuation (pages 97-103)

In this chapter Judith speaks of woundedness as an intrinsic and precious part of woman's individuation process. Were you surprised to read this? What is your understanding of this? Your experience of this?

Her return (pages 104-107)

This chapter ends with an image of wild geese as a symbol of the Feminine, with a woman responding to the wildness of their call. "After all the years of outer-directed energy, I am coming home to the Feminine . . . coming home to myself" (page 109). What image holds the symbol of the Feminine for you? What is your experience of "coming home"?

Her legacy (pages 108-113)

In this concluding chapter Judith describes the legacy women leave for each other. What legacy have you received from women of the past? From women in your family? From women who have influenced you in other areas of your life? How has their presence in your life made a difference? What is the legacy that you are leaving to your own daughters or nieces, to all women of the future?

❖ ❖ ❖

At the end of each section of this book, there is a two-page poem in which the earth murmurs, sings, and whispers her response. What is your response?